THE WISDOM OF ST JOHN OF THE CROSS

THE
WISDOM
OF
ST JOHN
OF THE
CROSS

Compiled and introduced by
Colin Thompson

LION
Giftlines

This edition copyright © 1999 Lion Publishing

Published by
Lion Publishing plc
Sandy Lane West, Oxford, England
www.lion-publishing.co.uk
ISBN 0 7459 3977 5

First edition 1999
10 9 8 7 6 5 4 3 2 1 0

A catalogue record for this book is available
from the British Library

Typeset in 12.5/13 Venetian 301
Printed and bound in Singapore

Artwork: Vanessa Card
Designer: Philippa Jenkins

Picture Acknowledgments

1: St John of the Cross, 1701 (engraving) by Spanish School (18th century)
Private Collection/Bridgeman Art Library, London/New York
2: St John of the Cross by Spanish School (16th century)
Private Collection/Bridgeman Art Library, London/New York
11: St Dominic by El Greco (1541–1614)
Toledo Cathedral, Castile, Spain/Bridgeman Art Library, London/New York
16: St John the Baptist in the Desert by Pedro Orrente (1588–1645)
Museo de Santa Cruz, Toledo, Spain/Bridgeman Art Library, London/New York
19: Christ in the Garden of Olives by El Greco (1541–1614), SuperStock Ltd
25: View of Toledo by El Greco (1541–1614)
Metropolitan Museum of Art, New York, USA/Bridgeman Art Library, London/New York
29, cover: The Saviour of the World, c. 1600 by El Greco (1541–1614)
National Gallery of Scotland, Edinburgh, Scotland/Bridgeman Art Library, London/New York
31: Christ Clasping the Cross by El Greco (1541–1614)
Prado, Madrid, Spain/Bridgeman Art Library, London/New York
35: Repentant Peter by El Greco (1541–1614)
Bowes Museum, Co. Durham, UK/Bridgeman Art Library, London/New York
45: The Penitent Magdalene, 1579 by Luis de Carbajal (1513–post 1613)
Museo de Santa Cruz, Toledo, Spain/Bridgeman Art Library, London/New York
47: The Holy Family by El Greco (1541–1614), SuperStock Ltd
48: The Eternal Father by Francisco de Zurbarán (1598–1664)
Museo de Bellas Artes, Seville, Spain/Bridgeman Art Library, London/New York

CONTENTS

INTRODUCTION

John of the Cross was born Juan de Yepes in 1542, in a village to the west of Avila, on the plains of Castile. His father and middle brother died when he was very young and his mother moved with her two surviving boys to the nearest city. They were economic refugees, members of the poorest class in the community, dependent on the charity of others for survival.

Juan was educated at a local orphanage school, then entered a Jesuit college, paying his way by working as a care assistant in a local syphilis hospital. Having decided to become a Carmelite, he was sent to study at Salamanca, Spain's foremost university. A crisis of vocation led him to abandon his studies after four years and consider joining the stricter Carthusians, but he was persuaded by Teresa of Avila to extend the reform she had begun among the Carmelite sisters to the friars. He devoted the rest of his life to the Order which came to be known as the Discalced (Barefooted) Carmelites.

In December 1577 he was abducted by Carmelite friars opposed to the reform and held in solitary confinement in Toledo until his escape in August 1578. This personal dark night was the seedbed of his writing. In prison he composed his first poems and over the next few years completed commentaries on three of them which enshrine his spiritual teaching – *The Ascent of Mount Carmel* and *The Dark Night of the Soul* (actually one work), *The Spiritual Canticle* and *The Living Flame of Love*. In 1591 he again fell into disfavour and was sent to a remote monastery, where he became ill. He died during the night of 13–14 December 1591. He was canonized in 1726 and proclaimed a Doctor of the Church in 1926.

His poems are passionate, sensual and intensely lyrical. Influenced by the Song of Songs, they use the language of human love to speak of the love between God and the human soul. His commentaries are difficult: his style is more analytical and less personal than Teresa of Avila's, and he uses many expressions familiar to philosophers and theologians of his own age but not to ours.

Perhaps because of the poverty and suffering of his early years and the simplicity and austerity of the life he chose, he insists on the need to walk in the way of the Cross and on cultivating a spirituality which is God-centred rather than self-indulgent. His most famous phrase, 'the dark night of the soul', symbolizes the whole of the spiritual journey. It begins within the self, where God is hidden, and is often painful and disturbing. The soul, or self, needs to be freed of wrong priorities and choices and remade through faith, hope and love. She must travel in the darkness of faith towards the divine darkness, but is not dependent on her own resources alone. As she journeys, she is given strength and grace to progress further. John is clear that the extraordinary phenomena which may occur, like visions and raptures, must be disregarded, because the goal of the journey is not strange experiences of uncertain status but transformation in the love of God.

John only negates to affirm something greater. If he writes of created things as a burden or an obstacle, it is not because he has an unhealthy suspicion of the physical world: his poetry shows delight in God's creation. The problem lies in the way we choose to use it. We need to be liberated from the possessive desires and habits which make us dependent on finite things, not so that we can do without them but so that they can be free to be themselves and be enjoyed for their own sake. Though John's teaching can seem individualistic, he writes from the experience of living in community and often insists on the need for love of neighbour. The soul should be seen as representative of any human being. He anchors his teaching in his reading of Scripture. He teaches a way which ends in the greatest of all joys, the union of the soul with God. The union his poems celebrate and his commentaries analyse is only a foretaste of the everlasting enjoyment of God beyond death. But it is the goal for which humanity was created.

In this selection we follow the journey from its first beginnings to fulfilment. The translations are mine. Sometimes I have adapted the extracts so that they can stand intelligibly on their own.

COLIN THOMPSON

THE
HIDDENNESS
OF GOD

THE LANGUAGE OF GOD

He is above the heavens and speaks in the ways of eternity; we are on earth and blind, and understand only ways of flesh and time.

The Ascent of Mount Carmel, 2.20.5

The greatest need we have is to be silent before our great God with our appetite and our tongue, for the language he hears best is silent love alone.

Sayings of Light and Love, 131

THE HIDDENNESS OF GOD

Oh, soul, most beautiful of all the creatures, desiring so much to know the place where your Beloved is, to seek him and be united with him! You yourself are the place where he dwells, his inner chamber and his hiding-place. What more do you desire, what else do you seek outside yourself, when you possess within yourself your riches and delights, your satisfaction, your fullness and your kingdom, your Beloved, whom your soul desires and seeks? Rejoice and be glad in your inner recollection with him, since he is so close. Desire him there, adore him there, and do not go looking outside yourself, for you will tire yourself and become distracted, nor will you find him or enjoy him more surely or more quickly than within yourself. But you should know one thing: though he is within you, he is hidden.

The Spiritual Canticle, 1.7–8

HIDDEN IN THE HIDDENNESS OF GOD

Since he whom my soul loves is within me, how is it that I can neither find nor experience him? The reason is that he is hidden and that you are not also hiding in order to find and experience him. Since you know that your longed-for Beloved dwells hidden in your heart, strive to be well hidden with him. Seek him in faith and in love, finding no satisfaction in anything else, for these are the two guides for the blind who will lead you by an unknown way to the hidden place of God. Faith provides the feet by which the soul goes to God, and love is the guide which directs her.

The Spiritual Canticle, 1.9–11

Seek by reading and you will find by meditating. Knock by praying, and it will be opened to you in contemplation.

Sayings of Light and Love, 157

THE HIDDEN FOUNTAIN

There is a fountain flowing
whose source is past my knowing
 although by night.
Yet from it all creation
drinks life and inspiration,
 although by night.

Its beauty, past comparing,
 refreshes the wayfaring,
 although by night.
Its depths are never sounded,
its treasures are unbounded,
 although by night.

Its brightness never darkens,
it calls whoever hearkens,
 although by night.
To all its voice is calling
who see the darkness falling,
 although by night.

Its ceaseless flow is singing
'At last the day is springing!'
although by night.
This healing stream, who knows it?
The Bread of Life bestows it
through the long night.

Based on 'How well I know the fountain'

The Depths of Mystical Wisdom

This mystical wisdom has the property of hiding the soul in itself. Sometimes it so absorbs and plunges the soul into its secret depths that she begins to see clearly how very distant and remote she is from every created thing. She seems to have been placed in the deepest and widest of lonely places, where no human being can reach, as if in an immense and boundless desert, yet the more pleasant, delightful and full of love the deeper, wider and lonelier it is. And these depths of wisdom so raise and ennoble the soul, so bring her to the heart of the science of love, that she comes to know how lowly and inadequate and in some ways inappropriate are all the words and expressions used in this life about divine things, and how impossible it is by any natural means, however loftily and wisely one speaks about them, to know or experience them as they are without the illumination mystical theology brings.

The Dark Night of the Soul, 2.17.6

WORRY NEVER HELPS

It is always pointless to become anxious and worried, because it never helps at all. So even if everything should come to an end and fall apart and even if everything should be against you and turn out contrary, it is pointless to worry, because this causes more harm than good. To bear everything with a calm and peaceful steadfastness not only brings many benefits to the soul but also helps her to reach a better judgment about these very adversities and to find an appropriate remedy for them.

The Ascent of Mount Carmel, 3.6.3

THE
DARK NIGHT

SETTING OUT

On a dark night,
inflamed with anxiety in love,
I went forth unnoticed,
oh happy fortune!
my house now being at rest.

'On a dark night', v. 1

There are three reasons why this journey of the
soul towards union with God may be called
night. The first is the place from which the
soul sets out, because she must deprive herself
of her appetites for worldly possessions. This
denial and privation is like night to the human
senses. The second is the road along which
she travels towards union, faith, which to the
human mind is also dark, like night. The third
is the destination, God, who is himself a dark
night in this life to the soul. These three nights
must pass through the soul, or rather, the soul
pass through them, to reach union with God.

The Ascent of Mount Carmel, 1.2.1

THE WAY OF DISPOSSESSION

To reach satisfaction in all
desire satisfaction in nothing.
To come to possess all
desire the possession of nothing.
To come to be all
desire to be nothing.
To come to the knowledge of all
desire the knowledge of nothing.
To reach what you do not enjoy
you must go by the way which shuns enjoyment.
To come to the knowledge you do not have
you must go by the way of not knowing.
To come to be what you are not
you must go by the way in which you are not.

The Ascent of Mount Carmel, 1.13.11

THE NARROW WAY

Always try to be inclined
not to the easiest, but to the most difficult;
not to the most pleasant, but to the most distasteful;
not to the most enjoyable, but rather to what
brings less enjoyment;
not to what is restful, but to what is wearisome;
not to what brings consolation, but rather to
the lack of consolation;
not to the most, but to the least;
not to the highest and most prized, but to
the lowliest and most despised;
not to what involves wanting something, but to
not wanting anything;
not to go about seeking the best of temporal things,
but the worst;
to desire to enter in complete nakedness and
emptiness and poverty in respect of
all that the world has, for the sake of Christ.

The Ascent of Mount Carmel, 1.13.6

CASTING OFF THE OLD HUMANITY

To reach this high mountain a change of clothing is needed. God will effect this, changing old garments for new, placing in the soul a new understanding of God in God, in which the old human understanding is left behind, and a new love for God in God, since the will is now unencumbered by its old human desires and pleasures, and infusing a new knowledge into the soul, now that the former knowledge and images have been put aside. He will make everything which belongs to the old humanity, the capacity of natural being, cease, and the soul will be clothed with a new, supernatural capacity in all her faculties, so that her once human action becomes divine. This is what is gained in the state of union, in which the soul serves only as an altar on which God is adored in praise and love, God alone present in her.

The Ascent of Mount Carmel, 1.5.7

11

LOSS AND GAIN

That night guided me
more surely than the midday sun
to where there waited for me
him whom well I knew
there where no one else appeared.

'On a dark night', v. 4

Although this blessed night darkens the spirit,
it does so only to give it light for all things.
Although it brings it low and makes it miserable,
it does so only to exalt and raise it. Although
it impoverishes it and empties it of all natural
possession and affection, it does so only that the
spirit can expand to taste and enjoy all things
above and all below, with a general liberty of
spirit in everything.

The Dark Night of the Soul, 2.9.1

GOD
IN
CREATION

LETTING GO

The soul acquires more enjoyment and
pleasure from created things when she lets
them go. They cannot truly be enjoyed if they
are regarded as property to be grasped. This
brings anxiety, which binds the spirit to the
earth and leaves no space for growth in the
heart. For such a reason pleasure clouds our
judgment like a fog, because we cannot will
to enjoy created things without the will to
possess them. To deny and to purge that kind
of enjoyment leaves the judgment clear as air
when mist dissolves. The soul who enjoys
something of created things but with the will
so bound neither has nor possesses anything;
rather they are in possession of her heart, so
that, like a captive, she suffers. But the soul
unattached to them is free of worries about
them, at prayer or away from prayer, and
quickly gathers a large spiritual harvest.

The Ascent of Mount Carmel, 3.20.2–3

READING THE BOOK OF CREATION

Oh woods and thickets
planted by the hand of the Beloved!
oh meadow all of green
spangled with flowers,
say if he has passed through you!

The Spiritual Canticle, v. 4

Now the soul begins to journey through contemplation and knowledge of created things to knowledge of her Beloved, their Creator. After the exercise of self-knowledge, this contemplation of the created order is the first step on the spiritual way towards knowledge of God, by contemplating his greatness and excellence as evident in them. The invisible things of God are made known to the soul through both the visible and invisible creation. In this song the soul addresses the created elements, asking them for her Beloved.

The Spiritual Canticle, 4.1

CLOTHED IN THE BEAUTY OF GOD

Pouring down numberless graces
he passed swiftly through these woods,
and, looking on them as he passed by,
with his face alone
left them clothed in beauty.

The Spiritual Canticle, v. 5

As St Paul says, the Son of God is *'the splendour of his glory and the figure of his substance'* (Hebrews 1:3). God looked on all things with the image of his Son alone, which endowed them with their natural being and gave them many natural gifts and graces and created them perfect and complete, as Genesis states: *'God looked on all that he had made, and behold, it was very good'* (Genesis 1:31). To look on them as very good was to create them very good in the Word, his Son. And not only did he endow them with their natural being and grace when he looked upon them. He left them clothed in

beauty, endowing them with supernatural
being, with the image of his Son alone, when
he became man, exalting humanity in the beauty
of God, and with humanity, all creatures, since
he was united with the nature of them all in
his human nature. And so in this uplifting of
the Incarnation of his Son and in the glory
of his resurrection in the body, the Father not
only beautified the creatures in part, but, we
may say, he left them entirely clothed in beauty
and dignity.

The Spiritual Canticle, 5.4

PRAISE THROUGH THE SENSES

I want now to give you a test by which you
may know when sensual pleasures are beneficial
and when they are not. Every time you hear
music or other things, and see pleasant sights,
and smell sweet fragrances, and enjoy pleasant
tastes and delicate touches, if the first reaction
is for the will to turn its knowledge and
affection to God and for that knowledge
to bring the will more enjoyment than the
sensual object which is its cause, that is a sign
that benefit has been gained from it and that
the senses are helping the spirit. Then the
senses can be used, because then they are
serving the purpose for which God created
them and gave them to us, that is, to love
and know him better through them.

The Ascent of Mount Carmel, 3.24.5

THE
WAY OF
THE CROSS

THE WAY OF THE CROSS

If at any time anyone – a superior or anyone else – should persuade you of a teaching which is easier and more comforting, do not believe it or embrace it, even if it is confirmed by miracles. Rather, practise penitence, more penitence, and detachment from all created things. And if you wish to come to possess Christ, never seek him without the Cross.

Letter 24

To enter into the riches of God's wisdom the gateway is the Cross, which is narrow, and those who desire to enter it are few, though those who desire the delights to which it leads are many.

The Spiritual Canticle, 36.13

CRUCIFIED WITH CHRIST

Oh souls that desire to walk safely and with
consolation in spiritual matters! If you but
knew how right it is for you to undergo
suffering to reach such safety and consolation,
and how impossible it is otherwise to reach
what the soul desires, only to go backwards!
Then you would never seek consolation from
God or from created things, but rather would
carry the cross, be nailed to it and desire there
to drink gall and pure vinegar; and would
count it bliss when you saw how dying thus
to the world and to yourselves, you would
live to God in delights of the spirit.

The Living Flame of Love, 2.28

CHRIST CRUCIFIED WITHIN

Truly devout people centre their devotion
principally on what is invisible, and need and
use few images, and then only those which
conform more to the divine than the human.
Nor is their heart fixed on those they do use:
if they are removed from them, they are very
little troubled, since they seek the living image,
which is Christ crucified, within themselves.

The Ascent of Mount Carmel, 3.35.5

TRANSFORMATION
IN
LOVE

GRACE OUR LOVING MOTHER

Once the soul has determined to be converted to the service of God, God nurtures her in spirit and caresses her, like the loving mother with her tender babe, warming it at her breasts, feeding it with nourishing milk and soft, sweet food, and carrying it in her arms and cherishing it. But as the child grows, its mother begins to withhold her caresses and to hide her tender love. She rubs bitter aloes on her sweet breast, puts the child down and lets it walk on its own feet, so that as it puts aside the behaviour proper to a babe, it can grow accustomed to greater and more substantial things. This is the work of our loving mother, the grace of God, in the soul.

The Dark Night of the Soul, 1.1.2

20

EQUALITY OF LOVING

For God to fall in love with the soul, he does not set his eyes on her greatness, but on the greatness of her humility.

Sayings of Light and Love, 102

What the soul aspires to is equality of love with God, because the lover cannot be satisfied if he does not feel that he loves as much as he is loved. The soul sees that though her love in this life is immense through her transformation in God, yet it cannot equal the perfection of God's love for her. So she desires clear transformation in glory, whereby she will reach such equality of loving… Her mind will then be God's mind, her will God's will, and so her love will be God's love. There she loves him as strongly and perfectly as he loves her, both wills being joined together in the one will and one love of God.

The Spiritual Canticle, 38.3

THE NIGHT OF LOVE

Oh night which guided!
Oh night more lovely than the dawn!
Oh night which joined
Beloved to the lover
the lover transformed in the Beloved!

'On a dark night', v. 5

Where there is no love, put love, and you will
receive love back.

Letter 27

EMPOWERED BY LOVE

This love is the end for which we were created. So let those who are very active and who think to span the world with their preaching and exterior works note that they would benefit the Church and please God much more if they spent even half the time with God in prayer. Then they would achieve more, and with less toil, by one work than they would with a thousand, through the merits of their prayer and having gained spiritual strength from it. Otherwise, it is all just hammering away, accomplishing very little, sometimes nothing at all, even sometimes causing harm. God forbid that the salt should lose its savour (Matthew 5:13)! Even when the soul seems to be engaged in some outward activity, this can achieve nothing substantial, because good works cannot be performed except by the power of God.

The Spiritual Canticle, 29.3

JOY IN THE BELOVED

My Beloved the mountains
the lonely wooded valleys
the strange islands
the sounding rivers
the whistling of the loving breezes,
the calm night
awaiting the rising of the dawn,
silent music
resounding solitude
the supper which brings recreation and love.

The Spiritual Canticle, vv. 14–15

POSSESSING ALL THROUGH THE BELOVED

Mine are the heavens and mine the earth.
Mine are the nations. The just are mine and
mine the sinners. The angels are mine and
the Mother of God and all things are mine.
And God himself is mine and for me, because
Christ is mine and wholly for me. So what
more do you ask and seek, my soul? All this
is yours and all is for you.

Sayings of Light and Love, 26

THE VISION OF CREATION RENEWED

How gently and lovingly
you awaken in my heart!

This awakening is a movement made by the
Word in the substance of the soul, of such
grandeur, majesty and glory, and so intimate
and gentle, that it seems to the soul that all
the balsams and fragrant spices and flowers in
the world are moving and mingling together
as they turn and give off their sweet fragrance;
that all the kingdoms and realms of the world
and all the powers and virtues of heaven are
moving; and that all the virtue and all the
substance, perfection and grace of every created
thing are shining as together they move, each
to the other and in the other. For as St John
says (1:3–4), *all things in him are life*; and as the
Apostle also says (Acts 17:28), *in him they live
and move and have their being.*

The Living Flame of Love, 4.4

THE BEAUTY OF CREATION SEEN IN CHRIST

Let us rejoice, Beloved,
and let us go to see in your beauty
the mountain and the hill
where the pure water flows;
let us enter further into the thicket.

The Spiritual Canticle, v. 36

In this awakening, all things reveal the beauties
of their being. For the soul here sees how all
the creatures, above and below, have their life,
duration and strength in him. Although it is
true that these things are distinct from God in
that theirs is a created being, she knows them
better in his being than in their own. And this
is the great delight of this awakening: to know
the creatures through God, not God through
the creatures; to know the effects through their
cause and not the cause through its effects.

The Living Flame of Love, 4.5

THE FLAME OF LOVE

Oh living flame of love!
how tenderly you wound me
in the deepest centre of my soul!

'Oh living flame of love', v. 1

This purifying, loving, divine knowledge or
light acts on the soul to purge it and dispose
it for perfect union with God in the way fire
acts on wood to transform it into fire. When
applied to wood, fire first begins to dry it
out, forcing its moisture out and making any
water it contains seep out. Then it starts to
blacken it, making it dark and ugly, even ill-
smelling. As it gradually dries it out, it begins
to be kindled, as all the ugly and dark accidents
which are contrary to fire are expelled from
the wood. Finally, as it begins to heat and
kindle it from without, it transforms it into
itself and makes the wood lovely as the fire.
That same light and loving wisdom in which
the soul will be united and transformed is

precisely what purifies and prepares her at
the outset. As the soul is purified and purged
in this fire of love, so she is more and more
inflamed in love, just as wood grows hotter
the more like fire it becomes.

The Dark Night of the Soul, 2.10.1, 3, 6

THE LIFE OF THE SOUL IN THE TRINITY

The breathing of the air,
the song of the sweet nightingale,
the grove and its graceful beauty
in the calm night,
with a flame which consumes, painlessly.

The Spiritual Canticle, v. 39

And it should not be thought impossible that
the soul can do so lofty a thing as breathe in
God through her participation in him as God
breathes in her. Given that God has honoured
her by uniting her with the most holy Trinity,
making her in the form of God and God
by participation, why should it be thought
incredible that she should be engaged in her
work of understanding, knowing and loving;
or rather that this be done in and together with
the Trinity, but through communication and
participation, as God works all this within her?

The Spiritual Canticle, 39.4

THE SUM OF PERFECTION

Forgetting all created things;
remembering the Creator;
attending to inward things;
and loving the Beloved.

Attributed to St John of the Cross

EXAMINED IN LOVE

In the evening you will be examined in love.

Sayings of Light and Love, 59